Look What You Can Make With

Boxes

Edited and designed by Lorianne Siomades
Photographs by Hank Schneider

Boyds Mills Press

Designer:

Lorianne Siomades

Production:

Rachel Bakota

Craftmakers:

Yvette Boucher   Nancy C. Duhaime

Paulette Carlson   Lorianne Siomades

Contributors:

Judy Burke   James W. Perrin Jr.

Jennifer Carling   Kathy Ross

Diane Cherkerzian   Constance Sharp

Laurie J. Edwards   Lorianne Siomades

Kathy Everett   Sharon Dunn Umnik

M. Mable Lunz   Colleen Van Blaricom

Carol McCall   Hilda K. Watkins

Beth Murray   D.A. Woodliff

Wanda Payne

Published by Bell Books
Boyds Mills Press, Inc.
A Highlights Company
815 Church Street
Honesdale, Pennsylvania 18431
Printed in China

Publisher Cataloging-in-Publication Data
Look what you can make with boxes: over 90 pictured crafts and dozens of other ideas /
edited by Lorianne Siomades ; photographs by Hank Schneider.—1st. ed.
[48]p. : Ill. ; cm.
Summary : Toys, games and other ideas all from boxes.
ISBN 1-56397-704-4
1. Handicraft—Juvenile literature. 2. Boxes—Juvenile literature.
[1. Handicraft. 2. Boxes.] I. Siomades, Lorianne. II. Schneider, Hank, ill. III. Title.
745.54—dc21   1998   AC   CIP
Library of Congress Catalog Card Number 97-76815

First edition, 1998
Book designed by Lorianne Siomades
The text of this book is set in 10pt Avante Garde Demi, titles 43pt Gill Sans Extra Bold

Getting Started

This book is filled with fun, easy-to-make crafts, and each one begins with a box. You'll find a wide variety of things to make, including toys, games, and gifts.

Directions

Before you start each craft, read the directions and look closely at the photograph, but remember—it's up to you to make the crafts your own. If we decorate a craft with markers, but you want to use glitter paint and stickers, go for it. Feel free to stray from our directions and invent new crafts.

Work Area

It's a good idea to keep your work area covered. Old newspapers, brown paper (from grocery bags), or old sheets work well. Also, protect your clothes by wearing a smock. A big, old shirt does the job and gives you room to move. Finally, remember to clean up when you've finished.

Materials

You'll need a lot of boxes, so start saving now. Ask friends and relatives to help. Keep your craft-making supplies together, and before making a craft, check the "You Will Need" list to make sure that you have everything. We often give suggestions for what kind of box works well for each craft. Also, since you'll need scissors and glue, tape, or a stapler for almost every craft, we don't list these supplies. (We do list craft glue—which is tackier than regular glue—when it helps to use it.)

Other Stuff

When we show several similar crafts, we'll often list numbered directions that apply to all of the crafts, then specific directions for each craft.

Free painting tip: Sometimes boxes have a shiny coating, and poster paint won't stick to them. Try mixing liquid soap with the paint. It works for us. You could also use acrylic paints.

That's about all. So, find a bunch of boxes, select a craft that you like, and have some fun. Before you know it, you'll be showing everyone what you made with boxes.

Little Box Safari

Set off to explore the wilderness . . . and keep your eyes open for tigers, hippos, and elephants!

You Will Need:

- various small boxes
- construction paper
- paints
- foam paper
- markers
- felt

More Ideas

Make an entire jungle scene with foam-paper rivers and waterfalls, papier-mâché hills, and box lions and turtles.

Or, select a different climate and create the animals that live there. Try making a desert scene, an Arctic scene, or an ocean scene.

To Invent an Animal

1 Paint a box or cover it with paper.

2 Cut out arms, legs, a tail, and other details from paper. Glue them on.

To Make the Lion

Paint a rectangular box. Cut out legs, a tail, and a head from foam paper. Glue them on. Add details with markers and cut foam paper.

To Make the Hippo

Paint a square box. Glue on foam-paper legs, a back, a tail, and a head. Add features with markers and cut paper.

Be on the lookout for all kinds of boxes, too. That's what you'll need to make these animals.

To Make the Tiger

Paint a box. Glue on legs, a tail, and a head cut from paper and felt. Add details with markers. Glue on felt stripes.

To Make the Monkey

Paint a box. Glue on cut-paper arms, legs, a tail, and a head. Add details with markers.

To Make the Elephant

Paint a flat rectangular box. Cut a body with legs on it from foam paper. Wrap it around the box and glue the sides to the box. Add a foam-paper trunk, ears, eyes, and toes. Add details with markers and cut paper.

To Make the Trees

Glue paper onto a rectangular box. Cut palm branches and coconuts from paper and glue them to the top.

Camera

Snap away the hours with a handmade toy camera.

You Will Need:
- paper cup
- box (pudding)
- plastic cap
- paints
- construction paper
- yarn

1 To make the lens, cut the bottom inch from the paper cup. Glue it to the box.

2 To make the shutter button, glue on the plastic cap. Paint the camera. Add cut-paper details.

3 Braid yarn to make a neck strap. Glue the ends to the sides of the camera.

More Ideas

Draw and color your own snapshots, and put them in an album.

Use a larger box to make a toy video camera.

Vacation Box

Keep games, postcards, and mementos in this box, and follow your travel route on the map.

You Will Need:
- extra map of your travel route
- box and lid (shoes)
- buttons
- hole punch
- yarn

1 Glue the map onto the box and lid. Put the part with your travel route on the lid, if it fits. Cut slits in two corners of the lid to make a long tab. Glue the tab to the box.

2 Glue a large button on a small button. Glue the small button to the front of the box. Punch a hole in the lid. Tie yarn through the hole. To close the box, wrap the yarn behind the button.

More Ideas

With a marker, trace your travel route on the map. See how many nearby towns, lakes, and rivers you can identify as you travel.

Keep a journal of things you do and sights you see on your trip.

Boxy Backpack

Take this backpack anywhere—it can hold toys, treats, books, and anything else you can't leave home without.

You Will Need:

- large box (cereal)
- paints
- felt
- button
- small boxes
- construction paper
- thick ribbon

More Ideas

Pack a lunch, throw it in your backpack, and get permission to go on a hike and a picnic.

Cover your backpack with aluminum foil and use it as part of an astronaut costume.

1 Cut the top from the box. Cut a V-shape in the front, and four horizontal slits in the back—two at the top, two at the bottom. Tape the bottom of the box closed. Paint the box.

2 Cut out a piece of felt with a V-shape on one edge to match the opening in the box. Glue the back and sides of the felt to the box. Cut a buttonhole in the bottom of the V. Glue a button on the box.

3 Cover small boxes with paper and glue them onto the sides and front of your backpack. Leave the tops off the boxes so that you can carry items in them. To make straps, weave two long pieces of ribbon through the slits in the back. Glue or tie the ends together inside the box.

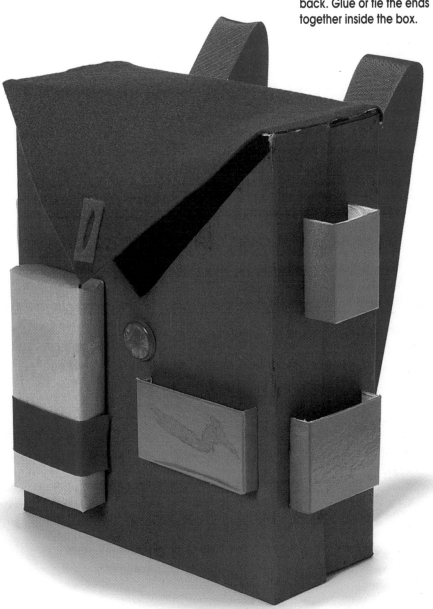

Super Shadow Boxes

Try your hand at creating a three-dimensional scene, then decorate a wall, shelf, or windowsill.

You Will Need:

- small boxes (greeting cards; gifts) or box lids (gifts; oatmeal)
- paints
- construction paper
- fabric
- string
- foam paper
- other items

1 Decorate a box or box lid with paints, cut paper, or fabric.

2 Follow the instructions for a particular shadow box, or create your own.

3 Glue string on the back as a hanger, or set it on a shelf.

To Make the Apple Tree Scene

Use paints and foam paper to create the sky, grass, and clouds in the box. Add a toothpick fence. Cut out the top and the trunk of a tree three times from paper. Glue them in the box, one on top of the other, with tiny pieces of foam paper in between to add depth.

To Make the Butterfly Box

Glue lace around an oatmeal-box lid. Paint uncooked bow-tie pasta pieces, and glue them in the box. Glue a piece of chenille stick onto each bow tie.

More Ideas

If you use a greeting-card box, glue on the clear cover after you've finished.

Make a series of shadow boxes to show the same scene during the four seasons. Or, make a shadow box for each month of the year.

Use a large shadow box as the background for a finger-puppet play.

Place objects or figures in different locations within the box—see how much depth you can add.

To Make the Pinecone Girl

Decorate a wooden ball to make the girl's head. Use rickrack as hair and a button as a hat. Add plastic wiggle eyes and colored-pencil features. Glue the ball on top of an upside-down pinecone. Add winged maple seeds as arms. Glue the girl in the box.

To Make the Diamond-Shaped Box

Glue silk or dried flowers into a thimble or a cap. Glue the arrangement into the box at an angle. Decorate the box with ribbon.

To Make the Winter Scene

Decorate the inside of the box with twigs and feathers. Add rickrack as the snow on the ground. Glue small toys or wooden cutouts onto buttons or plastic lids. Glue them into the box.

To Make the Flower Box

Cut a flower, a butterfly, and grass from foam paper. Glue them into the box.

Berry Hot!

These fruity trivets will protect your table from hot dishes—and add some zip at the same time.

You Will Need:

- corrugated cardboard box
- pencil
- rubber bands
- paints
- felt

1 Cut one side from the box. To make a base, draw the outline of a fruit shape on the cardboard and cut it out.

2 Cut 1-inch-wide strips of cardboard from the box. Put glue on each strip and wind it into a coil. Keep winding strips around the coil until the trivet is as large as you'd like. Use rubber bands to hold the strips in place until the glue dries. To make grapes, wind individual strips into coils and glue them next to each other on the cardboard base.

3 Paint the trivet. Cut details from felt. Glue them on.

More Ideas

Make a trivet to look like your favorite food. Basic shapes, such as a tomato, an ice-cream cone, or an eggplant, are easiest.

Dancing Butterflies

This is the simplest craft in the book to make, but one of the most fun to play with.

You Will Need:

- box with a clear plastic cover (greeting cards)
- paints
- tissue paper

1 Remove the cover from the box. Paint the inside of the box. Cut small figure-8-shaped pieces of tissue paper. Twist the centers of two together to make a butterfly. Make a few.

2 Place the butterflies in the box and put the cover on. Rub your finger quickly back and forth over the cover. Watch the butterflies dance!

More Ideas

Paint a background inside your box. Cut various flying creatures from tissue paper.

Frog Box

No matter what you keep in this box, it's sure to catch everybody's attention.

You Will Need:

- foam paper
- plastic box with an attached lid (baby wipes)
- plastic-foam ball
- paints
- plastic wiggle eyes

1 Cut arms and legs from foam paper. Glue them to the box. Cut the plastic-foam ball in half. Paint each half, and add a wiggle eye. Glue them to the box lid.

2 Paint on a mouth, and glue on a foam-paper tongue.

More Ideas

Use the frog box as a tackle box. Keep your fishing lures and flies in it.

Fun on the Farm

Build a barnyard, and have a hoedown with the horses, roosters, and other box creatures.

You Will Need:

- boxes of various sizes
- paints
- cardboard or foam board
- markers
- construction paper
- foam paper
- ruler

To Make the House

Turn a box sideways. Cut the corner from a larger box so that the triangular shape fits on top of the first box. Glue it in place. Glue a small box to the front of the house. Paint the house. Cut a roof from cardboard. Paint it, and glue it on. Add details with markers, cut paper, and foam paper.

To Make the Tractor

Paint a small box or glue paper on it. Cut four wheels from cardboard and four from foam paper. Glue the foam paper to the cardboard. Glue on the wheels. Add details with cut paper and foam paper.

To Make the Fence

Cut two long, half-inch-wide strips of cardboard, and many shorter strips of the same width. Lay the long strips parallel to each other. Connect them by gluing the shorter strips onto them.

Making each piece is fun, but the best part starts after you've finished the whole farm. Hee-haw!

To Make the Barn

Lay a big box on its side. Cut the corner from another box so that the triangular shape fits on top of the first box. If the bottom box is too wide for only one triangular shape, cut another. Glue on the triangular shapes. Paint the barn. Cut a roof from cardboard. Paint it, and glue it on. Add details with cut paper and markers.

To Make the Chicken

Cut out the head and neck from cardboard. Glue them onto a tiny box. Paint the chicken. Cut wings and a tail from foam paper. Glue them on. To make legs, cut a small strip of cardboard, bend it in half, then bend the ends as feet. Glue the legs to the bottom of the box.

To Make the Silo

Paint a cylindrical box or glue paper to it. To make the roof, cut a circle from foam paper. Cut a slit from the edge to the middle and overlap the edges of the slit. Glue the slit closed, then glue the roof on the silo. Add foam-paper details.

More Ideas

Make people for your farm, along with cows, horses, and pigs. Add a farm pond with ducks and swans.

To make a working farmhouse or barn, get some ideas from the dollhouses on pages 24 and 25.

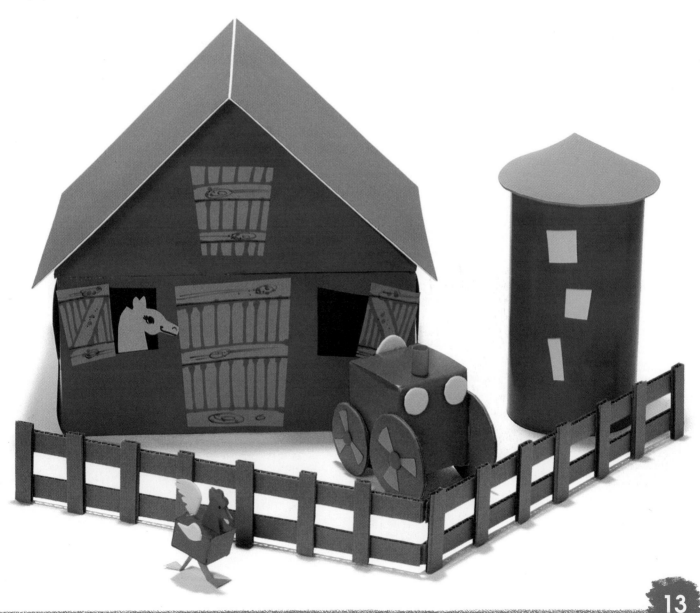

Piggy Bank

This little piggy will watch your coins.

You Will Need:

- construction paper
- square box (tissues)
- paper cup
- small box (pudding)
- wooden balls
- paints
- chenille stick
- markers

1 Glue paper over the hole in the tissue box. To make a nose, cut the bottom from the cup. Glue it to the pudding box. Glue the pudding box to the tissue box.

2 Glue on wooden balls as legs. Paint the pig. Cut a coin slot in the top.

3 Curl a chenille stick. Glue it in place as a tail. Add features with markers and cut paper.

More Ideas

Make an owl bank to remind you to save wisely.

Bookends

These clever bookends will blend right in with your book collection.

You Will Need:

- small stones or sand
- plastic bags
- boxes of various sizes
- paints
- construction paper
- markers

1 Put stones or sand in plastic bags. Close them with tape or twist ties. Put the bags in the boxes. Tape the boxes shut.

2 Paint the boxes, or glue paper to them. Add details with cut paper and markers.

3 Use them to hold books upright on a shelf.

More Ideas

Give these bookends as a gift to someone who loves to read.

Flying Butterfly Boxes

Let your imagination fly when creating this box mobile, then give it as a springtime gift.

You Will Need:

- large corrugated cardboard box
- small boxes
- paints
- construction paper
- markers
- hole punch
- yarn

More Ideas

Make a mobile to hang near a window. Use pictures of birds and flowers on the boxes.

Hang a bell from the bottom of each small box.

1 Cut a frame from the large box to hang the small boxes from. Paint the frame and the small boxes, or cover them with paper.

2 Cut butterflies from paper and glue them on the small boxes. Add details with markers.

3 Poke a hole in the top of each small box. Push a piece of yarn through it and glue it in place. Punch holes in the frame. Tie the yarn through the holes. Hang the mobile with yarn.

Big Box Band

Get some friends together and make your own musical box band. Instruments can be made from nearly any kind of box.

You Will Need:

- corrugated cardboard box
- paints
- hole punch
- jingle bells
- yarn
- boxes of various sizes
- chenille sticks
- rubber bands
- craft sticks
- pencil
- small plastic-foam ball
- fabric
- felt

To Invent an Instrument

1 Paint and decorate a box or a panel cut from a box.

2 Add a noisemaking feature, such as a rubber band to pluck, dried beans to shake, or a block of wood to strike.

To Make the Tambourine

Cut a strip of corrugated cardboard, bend it in a circle shape, and staple the ends together. Paint it. For each jingle bell that you want to attach, punch two holes in the cardboard. Tie on each jingle bell with yarn.

More Ideas

Make a maraca by putting dried beans in a small gift box and gluing it closed. Tape a craft stick to it as a handle.

Look around your house and see what other objects might work well as instruments. To make a gong, hit a baking pan with the striker. Turn a big can upside down, and use it as a drum.

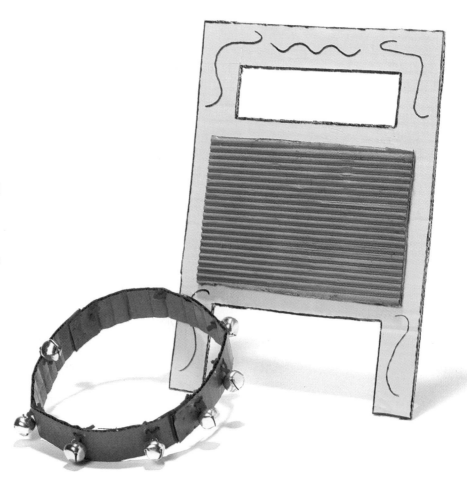

Percussion instruments are sounded by striking, scraping, or shaking—here's how to make one of each kind, plus a stringed instrument.

To Make the Washboard

Peel off the top layer from cardboard, exposing the corrugated part. Cut this part into a square, and paint it. Cut a larger piece of cardboard in the shape of a washboard, and paint it. Glue the corrugated square onto the washboard.

To Make the Banjo

Cut a large hole in a box, and punch three holes below it. Tape the top closed, and glue a long, rectangular box on it. Punch three sets of two holes in a small box. Thread a short chenille stick through each set of holes and twist the ends together inside the box. Glue the small box onto the rectangular box. Paint the banjo. Tie yarn or rubber bands from the chenille sticks to the holes in the large box.

To Make the Xylophone

Cut a corner of a shoe box and one of the long sides along the bottom, forming a long tab. Push the tab toward the middle of the box. Cut off the excess on the bottom. Glue the edges closed. Glue three craft sticks together, ends overlapping, so that they are slightly longer than the box. Repeat with three more sticks. Glue both long sticks to the box, then glue five craft sticks across them.

To Make the Striker

Glue the pointy end of a pencil into a small plastic-foam ball. Cut out a square piece of fabric. Wrap it around the ball, and hold it in place with a rubber band. Cut a square piece of felt. Wrap it around the ball, and hold it in place with another rubber band.

Cuckoo Boxes

Make a whole family of colorful cuckoos from boxes, feathers, and straws.

You Will Need:

- boxes of various sizes
- paints
- construction paper
- feathers
- markers
- plastic-foam balls
- plastic drinking straws

1 To make the body, paint a small box or glue paper on it. Glue on a tail and wing feathers.

2 To make the head, paint another box, or cut a head from paper. Decorate it with paints or markers. Glue it to the bird's body.

3 To make the base, cut a plastic-foam ball in half, and paint one half. Poke two holes in the bottom of the body. Paint two straws, and glue them in the holes as legs. Glue the legs into the base.

More Ideas

Decorate your box bird to look like a pink flamingo, an ostrich, or an emu. Or, make a turkey and use it as a Thanksgiving centerpiece.

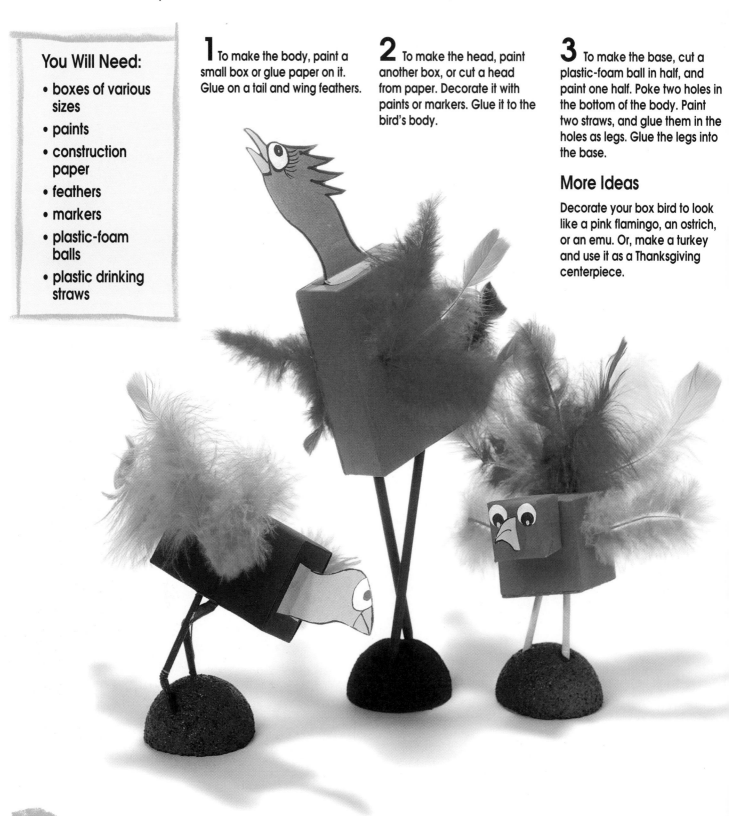

Recipe Box

Keep all of your favorite recipes together in a custom-made box.

1 Paint the box.

2 Cut food pictures from magazines and glue them on the box.

More Ideas

Make section dividers with tabs to separate recipes for different types of foods.

Have a recipe-trading party with friends. Have everyone bring his or her favorite food, then eat, make recipe boxes, and trade recipes.

You Will Need:

- box large enough to hold 4-by-6-inch cards
- paints
- pictures from old magazines

Fish Tank

Create an underwater world filled with plants and creatures.

1 Set the cover aside, and paint the inside of the box. Cut fish, seaweed, and other things from paper. Add tabs to the seaweed and other objects that will be connected to the bottom. Add details with markers.

2 Fold the tabs back and glue the objects to the bottom. Cut straw pieces. Glue one end of each piece to the back of a fish. Glue the other end to the back of the box.

More Ideas

If you want to make a large fish tank, use a large box, then use plastic wrap to cover the front when you've finished.

You Will Need:

- box with a clear plastic cover
- paints
- construction paper
- markers
- clear plastic drinking straws

Wacky Feet

These zany feet are funny to look at, but tricky to walk in. Be extra careful when trying them out!

You Will Need:

- corrugated cardboard boxes
- paints
- small boxes
- construction paper
- chenille sticks
- beads

1 Cut the basic foot shape from corrugated cardboard. Paint it.

2 Cut a section from a small box (large enough for your foot). Paint it or glue paper on it. Staple or glue it to the large foot.

3 Make another wacky foot. Put your feet in them. Carefully try to walk.

More Ideas

Hold a wacky-feet party for your friends, and use the feet as part of a costume.

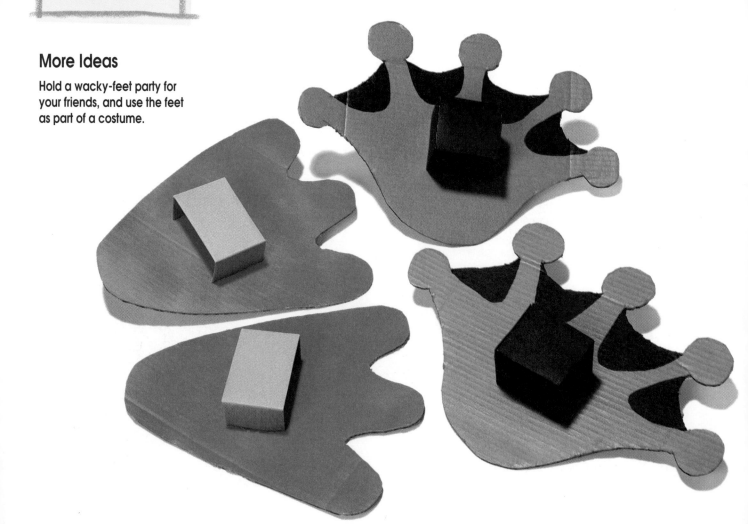

The trick to walking is to lift your knees high and keep your feet at a good distance from each other.

To Make the Duck Feet

Cut each foot in a triangle shape. Round off one point and cut three rounded toes in the opposite end.

To Make the Frog Feet

Cut each foot in a wide triangle shape. Round off one point and cut five webbed toes in the opposite end.

To Make the Pig Feet

Cut each foot in a teardrop shape, then cut a notch out of the point.

To Make the Clown Feet

Cut each foot in a pear shape. Glue on chenille-stick shoelaces and beads.

Scrapbook

Fill a scrapbook with your favorite photos and mementos.

You Will Need:

- thin cardboard box (cereal)
- paints
- pictures from old magazines
- hole punch
- paper
- yarn

1 Cut the front and back panels from the box, leaving part of the top flap attached to each panel. To create the cover, glue the flaps together.

2 Paint the cover and glue on pictures and letters or words cut from magazines. Punch matching holes in a stack of paper and in the cover. Tie the pages into the book with yarn.

More Ideas

Make a scrapbook for someone as a birthday gift. Include photos of the two of you, ticket stubs from events you attended together, and other keepsakes.

Funny Finned Friend

Hang up this creature and watch him flap in the breeze.

You Will Need:

- box (cereal)
- paints
- sponge
- construction paper
- plastic wiggle eyes
- yarn

1 Cut a long and a short corner from the box. Cut cardboard to fit over the open edges. Glue it in place. Glue the box corners together. Paint the box a light color. Let it dry. Dab on a darker color with a sponge.

2 Cut fins from paper and paint them. Glue them on. Add wiggle eyes. Tape yarn to the top of the creature so that it will hang straight. Once you find the right spot, poke a hole and glue the yarn in it.

More Ideas

Tie streamers onto your finned friend's tail, and use it as a windsock.

Campsite Diorama

Create a tiny world for your action figures or dolls. Play with it or use it as a decoration.

You Will Need:

- box (clothes)
- paints
- sand and stones
- plastic wrap
- construction paper
- twigs
- modeling clay

1 Cut the sides of the bottom of the box at an angle. The low part will be the front. Paint the box. Create a scene with sand, stones, and a stream made from painted plastic wrap.

2 Make trees and a campfire from cut paper and twigs. Stand the trees in lumps of clay. Make a tent from cardboard cut from the top of the box. Paint it and set it up in the scene.

More Ideas

Make a bead person by folding a piece of chenille stick in half, putting yarn in the fold, then pushing the ends of the stick through a bead. Add features with markers. Wrap another chenille stick around the body as arms.

Adorable Dollhouses

Playing with a dollhouse is fun, but it's even more fun when you've crafted it yourself.

1 The back of the house will be the bottom of a large box. Cut off all but three or four inches from the sides of the box. With a pencil, draw lines inside the box where the floors and room dividers will be.

2 Decorate the walls in each room by painting them or by gluing on wallpaper scraps or construction paper. Add cut-paper windows, curtains, and other wall decorations.

3 Use cardboard or foam board as floors and room dividers. Make each floor an inch longer than the width of the house. At each end, bend the floor down a half inch to form a tab. Put glue on the tabs, and glue the floor in place. Cut room dividers long enough to fit snugly between the floors. Glue them in place.

Decorating the rooms and making the furniture will really let you show your style.

4 Design a roof from cardboard or foam board. Glue or tape it in place. Decorate the roof and outside of the house with paint, markers, and construction paper. Create furniture from small boxes or sections from a longer box. Paint them, then decorate them with foam-paper details.

More Ideas

Make a list of what you like best about the place where you live, then create these features for your dollhouse. Chimneys and fireplaces, staircases and bookcases, bathtubs, or even hot tubs can help to personalize your doll's home.

Go beyond the house and make a garage, a swimming pool, a doghouse, or a mini-playground. Create an entire neighborhood!

Boxes in the Kitchen

A kitchen is home to many boxy appliances. Here's how to make a sink, an oven, and a refrigerator.

To Make the Fridge

Paint a box and lid. Cut shelves from cardboard or foam board. Make each shelf an inch longer than the width of the fridge. At each end, bend in the shelf a half inch to form a tab. Cover the shelves with paper. Put glue on the tabs, and glue the shelves in place. Cut the end off another box to make the snack drawer. Decorate it, and slide it into the fridge. Tape the side of the lid onto the box as the door. Glue on a foam-paper handle.

To Make the Sink

Cut a rectangular hole in the bottom of a box. Turn the box over. Glue cardboard or foam board on the back so that it stands up higher than the box. Cut two doors in the front panel. Paint the sink and decorate it with beads and foam-paper details. To make faucets, glue craft-stick pieces onto plastic caps. Paint them and glue them on the sink.

To Make the Stove

Turn a box upside down. Glue cardboard or foam board on the back so that it stands up higher than the box. Cut a door in the front panel. Paint the stove and decorate it with foam-paper details, beads, and markers.

More Ideas

Make a microwave, a toaster oven, a washer and dryer, a desk, or a stereo system.

Make mini-appliances to fit in a dollhouse. Use smaller boxes, and adapt the directions and supplies where necessary.

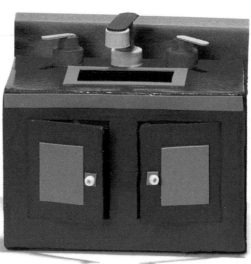

Marble Maze

Grab a stopwatch and challenge your friends to a marble-maze race.

You Will Need:

- large box
- construction paper
- markers
- marble

1 Decorate the box with construction paper and markers.

2 Cut a hole in one side to pop the marble through when starting the game. Cut a hole in the bottom at the opposite end for the finish.

3 Spread glue on paper. Roll it into a tube. Cut this into shorter tubes. Glue them in the box to form a maze.

More Ideas

Make dead ends by placing tubes against the sides of the box. Add other obstacles, such as trapdoor holes.

Picture Frame

This attractive, easy-to-make frame is a great place to display your favorite photos.

You Will Need:

- small box and lid (jewelry; gifts)
- wallpaper scraps
- craft glue
- ribbon
- photographs

1 Glue wallpaper scraps on the outside of the box and lid, and ribbon on the inside.

2 Join the edges of the box and lid together by gluing on two pieces of ribbon as hinges. Glue a photograph in each side of the frame.

More Ideas

Add a message and use it as a photo greeting card. Or, place a small gift inside and make it an all-in-one card and gift.

Boxcar Train Set

Get on board and create an entire railroad scene—trains, tunnels, buildings, and bridges.

You Will Need:

- ruler
- boxes of all sizes
- cardboard
- paints
- construction paper
- plastic drinking straws
- old magazines
- small paper cup
- pompons
- chenille sticks

1 Tape each box closed. Paint the boxes, or glue construction paper over them.

2 Follow the instructions for the craft you're making.

To Make the Tunnel

If using a tissue box, glue cardboard over the hole in the top before you paint it. Cut two arch-shaped holes on opposite sides of the box. Cut trees from paper. Glue them to the sides of the tunnel.

More Ideas

Make a floor scene for your train set. On poster board or an old sheet, draw train tracks, fields, and roads. Use aluminum foil to make a reflecting pond or river. Create pine trees by bending and stapling paper-plate halves into cones.

Experiment with different types of train cars. Make open-topped coal cars or birthday-express cars filled with presents.

Almost any box will do. We used boxes from toothpaste, tissues, soup, cereal, oatmeal, and raisins.

To Make the Buildings

Paint windows, doors, and other details on the boxes. Design a roof, cut it from cardboard, and glue it on. A corner cut from a larger box can be used as a roof.

To Make the Bridge

Cut the top three inches from a cereal box. Cut two strips of cardboard as wide as the top of the box. Tape them at each end of the top of the box. Cut an arch in the front and back of the bridge. Paint on details.

To Make the Water Tower

Remove the lid from an oatmeal container, and turn it upside down. To make the support poles, cut four rectangles from the open end of the container, leaving about an inch between them. To make the roof, cut a half-circle from paper, bend it into a cone shape, and glue it to the top. Glue on a drainage pipe cut from a straw.

To Make the Train

Add windows with passengers by cutting out faces from magazines or drawing your own. Glue them on. Cut wheels from cardboard and paint them. Glue two straw pieces to the bottom of each car, then glue the wheels onto the straw ends. Add details, such as a paper-cup smokestack and a cardboard-and-pompon headlight on the locomotive. Connect the cars with chenille sticks taped or glued in place.

Jewelry Box

Bangles, beads, and baubles—where to keep them all? Here's the answer.

You Will Need:

- large, flat box (candy)
- small boxes (jewelry; gifts)
- paints
- foam paper
- construction paper
- small mirror

1 Paint all the boxes and their lids, inside and out. Arrange the small boxes and lids inside the large box. Glue them in place.

2 Add details inside the boxes with paper. Glue the mirror inside the lid.

More Ideas

Replace the mirror with a small calendar, and use the box as a desk organizer.

Keep track of tiny craft supplies, such as beads, pompons, and sequins. Or, use it as a sewing box.

Happy House Doorstop

Open your door and welcome friends with a house doorstop.

You Will Need:

- large box (cereal)
- paints
- construction paper
- stones
- cardboard or foam paper

1 Cut the top two corners from the box, so that it's shaped like a house. Paint the box, and glue on cut-paper windows and a door.

2 Place stones inside the box, then glue a cardboard or foam-paper roof over the hole in the top of the box.

More Ideas

Decorate your doorstop to look like a small-scale version of the building where you live. Or, use a tiny box and make a house paperweight.

Fire Truck and Station

Here's a fire truck that's ready for rescue. You can also make a station to park it in.

You Will Need:

- five boxes (crackers; four smaller ones)
- paints
- construction paper
- foam paper
- twine

To Make the Fire Station

Cut the flaps from one end of a cracker box. Glue a smaller box to the side as the hose tower. Paint the fire station. Cut windows and other details from construction paper and foam paper. Glue them on.

To Make the Fire Truck

Glue two small boxes to the end of a long rectangular box. Paint the truck shape. Cut wheels, ladders, and other details from foam paper. Glue them on. Roll up some twine, and glue it on the truck.

More Ideas

Make a car that fits in a garage, a plane that fits in a hangar, or a train that fits in a roundhouse. Or, try making a stacking box puzzle with several boxes that fit inside one another.

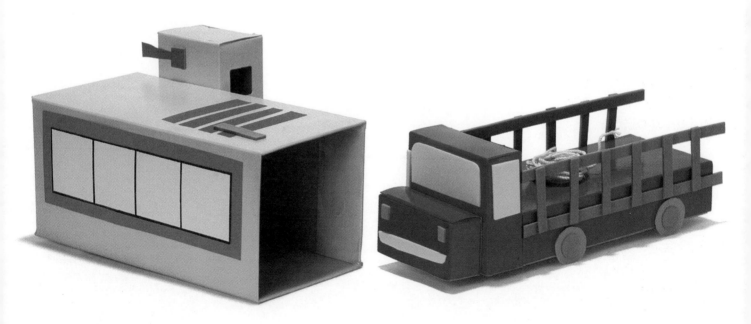

A Bunch of Box Games

Whether you like shooting hoops, tossing coins, or going fishing, you can find a way to make your favorite game with boxes.

1 Paint each box, or glue construction paper onto it.

2 Follow the instructions for the game you're making.

To Make the Coin Toss

Decorate boxes of various sizes with stickers. Paint a point value on each box: give boxes with large openings a low point value, and boxes with small openings a high point value. To play, arrange them on the floor. Each player tries to toss three coins into the boxes. The player with the highest score wins.

To Make the Basketball Hoop

Cut a backboard from foam paper or construction paper. Decorate it with markers, and glue it onto a box. Cut the bottom from a plastic cup. Glue or tape the cup to the bottom of the backboard. Use a table-tennis ball as a basketball.

When the competition begins, you can even keep score on a boxy scoreboard.

To Make the Fishing Game

Cut several slits in a box. From poster board, cut out a fish with a tab on the bottom, and punch a hole in the top. Decorate it with paints, markers, and beads. Make several. Stick them in the slits. To make a fishing pole, tie yarn and a bent paper clip to a stick or dowel.

To Make the Scoreboard

To make team-name hooks, poke two holes about 6 inches apart on the front of a box, toward the top. From inside the box, thread a chenille stick through the holes so that each end sticks out. Curl the ends into hooks. To make score hooks, poke two holes about 2 inches apart below each team-name hook. Thread a chenille stick through each set of holes, as before. From construction paper, make team-name cards and four sets of number cards from 0 to 9. Punch a hole in each. Make a "scoreboard" sign from foam board. Decorate it with markers, stickers, and foam paper. Glue it to the top of the scoreboard.

More Ideas

Create a bowling game with pins made from quart-sized milk cartons. Make a soccer game by cutting a plastic berry basket in half, and attaching the halves, or goals, to opposite ends of a large gift-box lid. Use crumpled foil as a ball.

Puppet Theater

Design your own puppet theater, and have a blast putting on puppet shows for your friends.

You Will Need:

- large corrugated cardboard box
- ruler
- paints
- construction paper
- markers
- foam paper

1 Cut off the back of the box, leaving a 1-inch border. Cut a square section from the front of the box, leaving a larger border.

2 Paint the theater. Make curtains and a sign from paper. Decorate them with markers.

3 From foam paper, cut a ruffle and tiebacks. Glue the curtains, ruffle, tiebacks, and sign onto the theater.

More Ideas

Make your own puppets (see pages 36 and 37), and write your own scripts.

Play television by decorating the box to look like a TV and putting your head behind it.

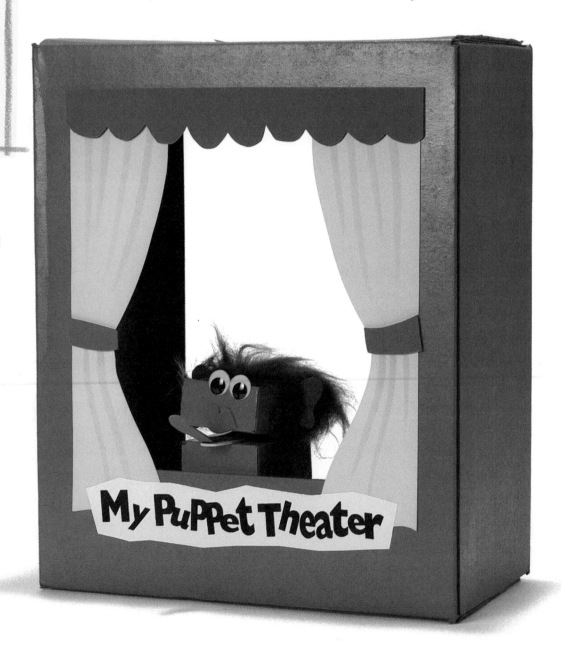

My Puppet Theater

Mailbox

Here's a place for your messages when you're not in your room.

You Will Need:

- box (shoes)
- foam paper
- cardboard
- craft stick
- metal paper fastener

More Ideas

Make a play tent for toys or dolls using the same shape, but replace the front with tent flaps.

1 Cut the box, as shown, with a door in one end.

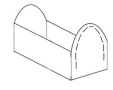

Cut on dotted line

2 Glue foam paper over it so that it forms a round top. Cover the front and back of the mailbox, too. Glue a foam-paper handle and a sign on the door.

3 Make a flag and a holder from cardboard and a craft stick. Put a paper fastener through the holder, the bottom of the flag, and the mailbox. Put the flag up when you have mail.

Box Baskets

Keep anything from food to flowers in these decorative baskets.

You Will Need:

- corrugated cardboard boxes
- paints
- fabric
- toothpicks or craft sticks
- cardboard
- metal paper fasteners

1 Cut off the top flaps, then paint the boxes or cover them with fabric. Add details, such as a fence made from toothpicks or craft sticks.

2 Make a handle from cardboard. Glue it on, or attach it with paper fasteners.

More Ideas

Leave two flaps on top, if you wish to cover whatever's inside. Fill a basket with gift items, and use it as a present.

Playful Puppets

These goofy puppets will liven up any puppet show—grab some boxes and make a whole cast.

You Will Need:

- boxes of various sizes
- paints
- construction paper
- foam paper
- plastic wiggle eyes
- fake fur
- plastic-foam balls

1 Make the basic puppet. Paint it or glue on construction paper or foam paper.

2 Follow the instructions for the puppet you're making.

3 Put your hand in the puppet to make it talk or fly.

To Make the Basic Puppet

If you're using a long, narrow box, glue on the lid if it has one. Find the center and cut one long side and both short sides (almost cutting the box in half). Fold the box on the uncut side.

If you're using two boxes, tape them shut at one end. Cut off the flaps at the open ends, then make a hinge to connect the boxes by taping them or by gluing on paper.

Stretch your imagination. Try making these, or invent some silly creatures of your own.

To Make the Monster

Glue on wiggle eyes and fake fur. Cut out and glue on ears, a mouth, and a tongue from foam paper.

To Make the Crocodile

Glue wiggle eyes onto plastic-foam-ball halves. Make paper eyelashes and a tongue, and foam-paper teeth and nostrils. Glue them on.

To Make the Butterfly

Decorate the wings with cut-paper shapes. To make the body, roll foam paper or construction paper into a tube. Glue it on. Add a plastic-foam-ball head decorated with foam-paper features.

More Ideas

Birds, bears, lions, or lizards can all be made by following the basic instructions then adding different details. Make the puppet theater on page 34 and entertain your family and friends.

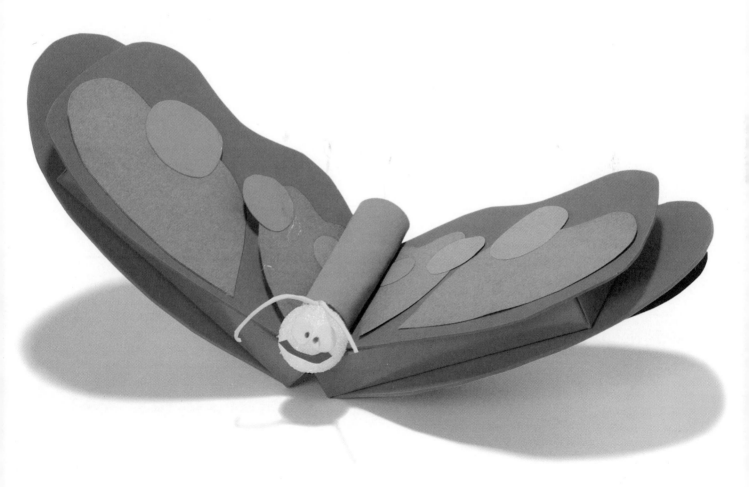

Elephants Never Forget

. . . to write back! Here's a great way to keep your paper and envelopes handy to write to your pen pal.

1 Cut the tops from the boxes. Paint the bottom parts, then glue them together.

2 Cut an elephant's head, ears, eyes, nose, and tail from paper. Glue the head on the front of the holder and the tail on the back.

3 To make legs, paint four paper cups and glue them on.

More Ideas

Use it to hold anything from new craft supplies to old greeting cards. Or, give it to an adult to use as a file box.

You Will Need:

- three cardboard boxes (cereal; cake mix)
- paints
- construction paper
- small paper cups

Keepsake Box

Favorite jewelry, tiny toys, or dried flowers are just a few of the treasures you can keep in this box.

1 Paint the box and lid. Cut shapes from foam paper.

2 Arrange the shapes and beads in a design on the lid. Glue them in place.

More Ideas

Decorate the box with natural materials, such as shells, dried beans, and seeds.

Put a small present inside and use it as a gift box that you don't have to wrap.

You Will Need:

- box and lid
- paints
- foam paper
- beads

Terrific Tiles

These tiles are fun to make, long lasting, and will look great anywhere in your house.

You Will Need:

- box lid
- modeling clay
- ruler
- objects to press into the clay
- plaster of paris
- paints

1 Cover the inside bottom of the lid with a half-inch layer of clay. Press objects into the clay to make a design, then remove the objects.

2 Following the directions on the plaster of paris container, mix up a batch and pour it into the lid so that it's about a quarter-inch deep.

3 When the plaster dries, take it out of the lid, remove the clay, and paint the tile.

More Ideas

Before the plaster dries, press objects such as dried beans and walnut shells into it and leave them there. You'll have designs on both sides of the tile.

Make a welcome plaque for your house. If you want to make letters, write them in mirror image. Place a hanging hook into the edge of the plaster before it dries.

Instead of using clay as your base, press objects into wet sand, then remove them and add the plaster of paris. It'll look like a sand sculpture.

Boxes on the Go!

By boat, by truck, by racecar, by bus—make all of your traveling toys from boxes.

You Will Need:

- boxes of all sizes
- paints
- construction paper
- foam paper
- cardboard
- plastic drinking straw
- ruler
- plastic lids
- markers
- milk carton
- small cardboard tubes
- cotton

1 Tape the boxes closed. Paint them or glue on construction paper or foam paper.

2 Follow the instructions for the craft you're making.

To Make the Truck

Glue together a rectangular box and a smaller box. Cut wheels from cardboard. Paint them, and glue them on the truck. Paint a straw, and glue it between the boxes. Cut details from foam paper and construction paper, and glue them on.

To Make the Car

Lay a box on its side, and cut a U-shaped hole in the top. To make the windshield, fold and glue the flap that you cut. To make the seat, cut a U-shape from foam paper. Glue it in the hole. To make the spoiler, cut a cardboard rectangle about 2 inches longer than the width of the car. Fold each end in one inch, and glue the ends to the sides of car, toward the back. Use painted plastic lids as wheels. Add details with markers and foam paper.

The more you make, the more fun it becomes. Soon you'll be making fleets of vehicles.

To Make the Bus

Cut wheels from cardboard. Paint them, and glue them on the bus. Add windows and other details with markers and cut paper.

To Make the Bulldozer

Cut a section from a cardboard tube, paint it, and glue it to the front of a box. Cut windows in a smaller box. Glue the smaller box onto the larger box. Add foam-paper details.

To Make the Boat

Cut and tape one end of a large rectangular box so that it forms a point, or use a milk carton. Cut a smaller box at a slant. Cut a window in each side, and glue it onto the larger box. Cut a cardboard tube at a slant, paint it, and glue it to the top of the boat. Add painted cotton as steam and other details cut from foam paper and construction paper.

More Ideas

To float the boat, glue it on a plastic-foam tray.

To make wheels that turn, poke a hole in the center of each wheel and in the places on the vehicle where each wheel will go. Attach the wheels with metal paper fasteners.

Make a racetrack and several cars. Or, create a larger town scene with a river, roads, and a construction site—places to put all of your vehicles.

Big Box Car

Drive this car anywhere—through the living room, across the backyard, or down the sidewalk. It doesn't need gas and it won't get a flat.

You Will Need:

- large corrugated cardboard box
- cardboard
- paints
- construction paper

1 Cut the bottom from the box. On the top, glue the two long flaps inside the box. To make the spoiler, fold back one of the short flaps and glue it in place.

2 To make the hood, tape or glue the other short flap to the sides of the car. Cut wheels and other details from cardboard, and glue them on. Paint the car, then add cut-paper details.

More Ideas

Make a horse, an airplane, a dinosaur, or anything you'd like to ride or drive.

Tie two strings onto the car and hang them over your shoulders.

Have a friend make one, and drive around together.

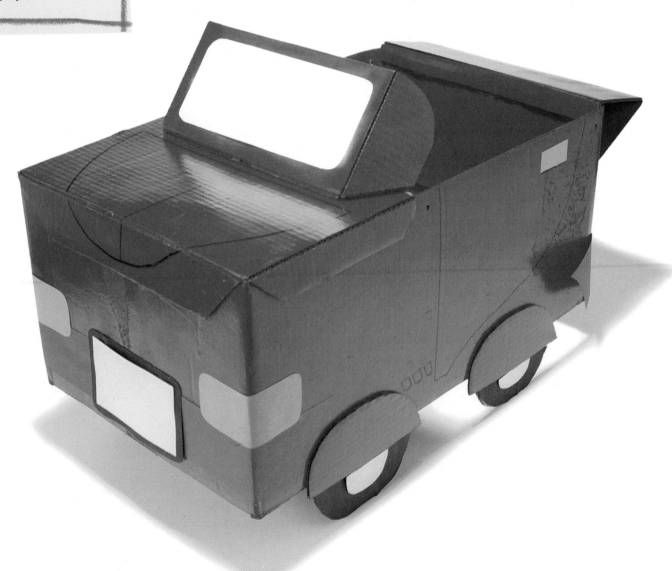

Kangaroo Keeper

This handy kangaroo's pouch can hold a lot more than her joey. There's plenty of room for books and some magazines, too.

You Will Need:

- large box (cereal)
- pencil
- paints
- construction paper
- fabric
- markers

1 Cut the top from the box. With a pencil, draw the basic outline of a kangaroo's head and pouch on both sides. Cut along the line.

2 Paint the box. Cut details from paper and fabric, and glue them on. Add features with markers.

More Ideas

Instead of a kangaroo, make a koala or an opossum. Or, design the sides to look like your favorite book or magazine.

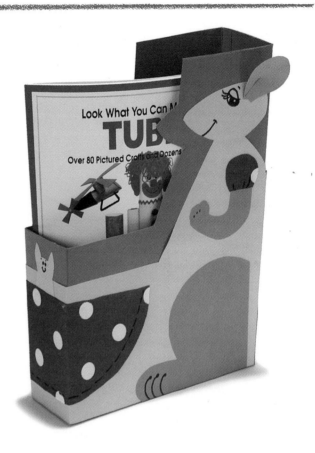

Message Board

This happy character will pass along important messages.

You Will Need:

- corrugated cardboard box
- craft glue
- fabric
- poster board
- markers
- construction paper

1 Cut two rectangles the same size from the box. Glue one on top of the other. Glue fabric over one side, and poster board on the other.

2 From poster board, cut a head, hands, and feet with a tab on each. Glue them to the message board, along the edges. Add details with markers and cut paper.

More Ideas

Design it to look like a mail carrier or a pony-express horse.

Rolling Box Buddies

Once you start making these, you'll really get rolling. Make a bunch, and give them as gifts.

You Will Need:

- boxes (shoes; cake mix)
- paints
- twine
- corrugated cardboard
- fabric
- construction paper
- metal paper fasteners
- felt
- cotton balls
- plastic wiggle eyes
- foam paper
- glitter
- markers

1 To make the body, turn a shoe box upside down, and paint it. To make the head, paint a smaller box and glue it on. Poke a hole in the front of the body. Thread twine through it, then tie a knot at both ends.

2 Cut wheels from cardboard, and glue fabric or construction paper on them. Poke a hole in each wheel, and holes in the body where the wheels will go. Attach the wheels with paper fasteners.

3 Follow the directions for the craft you're making.

These cooperative pets will follow you anywhere. Plus, they don't cost a penny to care for.

To Make the Lamb

Cut legs and ears from felt and glue them on. Then, glue painted cotton balls all over the head and body. Add wiggle eyes, a foam-paper nose, and a glittery mouth.

To Make the Duck

Cut wings and a tail from construction paper. Decorate them with markers, and glue them on. Add a foam-paper beak, wiggle eyes, and cut-paper eyelashes.

To Make the Dog

Cut spots from fabric, and other features from paper. Glue them on. To make the tail, cut fringe in a wide strip of paper, curl it up, then glue it on.

More Ideas

Leave the shoe box right side up to make an all-in-one wagon-pet. You can cut a notch in the bottom of the head to attach it to the body. Make a wagon-pet from a large box, and use it as a portable toy box.

Lion and Cage

Let this likable lion hang around in his cage or wander out for a stroll.

1 Cut a side panel from a large box. Glue the lid on. Cut a square in the front panel. Paint the cage. Glue on painted straws as bars.

2 Cut a smaller box in half lengthwise. Glue construction paper on it. Glue it inside the cage as a stand for the lion.

3 Fold paper in half and cut out the shape of a lion's body. Use paper, foam paper, and markers to make a tail, a mane, and a head. Add wiggle eyes.

More Ideas

Make an entire zoo, or a circus train, where each train car holds an animal.

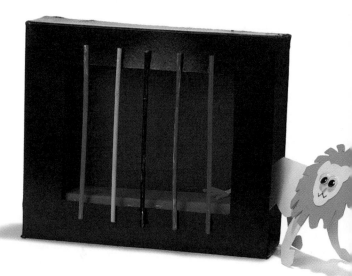

Secret Treasure Chest

We're not going to tell you what to keep in this chest. (Then it wouldn't be a secret!)

1 Cut the top from poster board. Glue it to the front and back of the lid. On poster board, trace around the half-circle shapes at each end of the lid. Cut them out, and glue them on.

2 To attach the lid to the box, cut a slit at each back corner of the lid to make a long hinge. Put glue on the inside of the hinge, and glue it to the box. Decorate the chest with cut-paper details.

More Ideas

Make a large chest for blanket or sweaters.

Make a secret panel underneath the lid.

Building Box Cards

You're the architect here—build countless creations with these easy-to-make cards.

1 Cut as many cardboard rectangles as you like. Make them all the same size.

2 Cut six slits in each card—two on each long side, one on each short side. Make them in the same places on each card.

3 Paint the cards, and build away!

More Ideas

Experiment with building cards of different shapes—triangles, circles, and hearts can work.

Title Index

Subject Index